CULTURE IN ACTION

Preening, Painting, and Piercing

Body Art

John Bliss

Chicago, Illinois

www.heinemannraintree.com
Visit our website to find out more information about Heinemann-Raintree books.

To order:

☎ Phone 888-454-2279

🖰 Visit www.heinemannraintree.com to browse our catalog and order online.

Edited by Louise Galpine, Megan Cotugno, and Abby Colich
Designed by Ryan Frieson
Original illustrations ©Capstone Global Library, Ltd.
Illustrated by Cavedweller Studio, Randy Schirz
Picture research by Liz Alexander
Originated by Capstone Global Library, Ltd.
Printed and bound in China by China Translation & Printing Services, Ltd.
14 13 12 11 10
10 9 8 7 6 5 4 3 2 1

Library of Congress Cataloging-in-Publication Data
Bliss, John.
  Preening, painting, and piercing : body art / John Bliss.
    p. cm. -- (Culture in action)
  Includes bibliographical references and index.
  ISBN 978-1-4109-3924-1 (hc)
  1. Body marking--Juvenile literature. 2. Body painting--Juvenile literature. 3. Body art--Juvenile literature. I. Title.
  GN419.15.B58 2010
  391.6--dc22
                    2009051182

Acknowledgments

The author and publishers are grateful to the following for permission to reproduce copyright material:

We would like to thank the following for permission to reproduce photographs: Courtesy of The Advertising Archives p. 10; Alamy pp. 4 (© Deco), 5 (© lemonlight features), 6 (© Mary Evans Picture Library), 9 (© imagebroker), 24 (© Pictorial Press Ltd), 25 (© F1online digitale Bildagentur GmbH), 27 (© Mihaela Ninic), 28 (© Mira); Corbis pp. 8 (© The Gallery Collection), 11 (© WAEL HAMZEH/epa), 14 (© Hans Georg Roth), 22 (© Marco Cauz), 23 (© Diego Azubel/epa); Getty Images pp. 7 (Sean Gallup), 12 (The Bridgeman Art Library/French School), 15 (William Thomas Cain), 26 (Scott Olson); Shutterstock pp. 16 (© gmwnz), 17 (© Dallas Events Inc), 18 (© Diane Gonzales), 20 (© Knud Nielsen).

Cover photograph of woman's hands and feet painted with henna reproduced with permission of Photolibrary (Vivek Sharma/Asia Images).

We would like to thank Jackie Murphy for her invaluable help in the preparation of this book.

Every effort has been made to contact copyright holders of any material reproduced in this book. Any omissions will be rectified in subsequent printings if notice is given to the publisher.

All the Internet addresses (URLs) given in this book were valid at the time of going to press. However, due to the dynamic nature of the Internet, some addresses may have changed, or sites may have changed or ceased to exist since publication. While the author and Publishers regret any inconvenience this may cause readers, no responsibility for any such changes can be accepted by either the author or the Publishers.

Author

John Bliss is a writer and teacher who teaches courses in theater and communication.

Literacy consultant

Jackie Murphy is Director of Arts at the Center of Teaching and Learning, Northeastern Illinois University. She works with teachers, artists, and school leaders internationally.

Contents

Many Kinds of Body Art 4

Centuries of Body Decoration. 6

The Magic of Makeup and Hair 10

Body Painting. 16

Tattooing 22

Piercing. 24

The Other Side of Body Art. 26

Looking to the Future. 28

Glossary *30*

Find Out More *31*

Index *32*

Important note:

Tattooing and piercing can be very dangerous. They should only be done by people who are trained to perform them safely. NEVER get a tattoo or piercing without permission from your parent or guardian.

Some words are printed in bold, **like this**. You can find out what they mean by looking in the glossary on page 30.

Many Kinds of Body Art

People around the world love to show off. They may do this through the clothes they wear or how they cut their hair.

Many people also decorate their bodies. For example, they may get a **tattoo** or have their ears **pierced**. These decorations are usually **permanent**— they last forever. Other kinds of body art, such as makeup and body paint, can be washed away. The ways people decorate their bodies, and the reasons they do so, have changed over the years. But almost every **culture** practices some kind of body art.

This native warrior from Papua New Guinea paints his face before going into battle. The paint is meant to frighten his enemy.

Why do people do it?

People decorate their bodies for many reasons. Some people do it as part of a **ceremony**, or special event. Others want to feel more beautiful. Sometimes it is a way to show something about people's personality.

Some people decorate their bodies in different ways for different reasons. For example, a woman might have a tattoo to show that she is a member of a group, but wear makeup to feel more attractive.

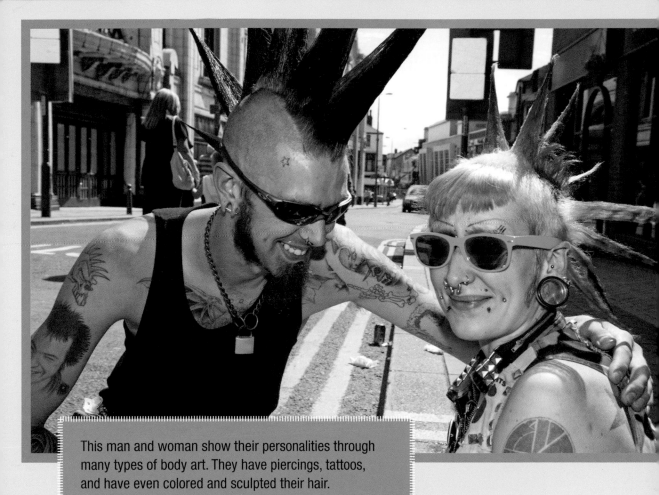

This man and woman show their personalities through many types of body art. They have piercings, tattoos, and have even colored and sculpted their hair.

The oldest tattoos?

In 1991 climbers found the body of a man frozen in the ice of the Alps Mountains. He was more than 5,000 years old. The man had 57 tattoos, which were made out of **soot** from a fire. Many of the tattoos were placed near joints where people suffer from a pain called arthritis. Because of this, scientists think these tattoos may have been meant to heal pain.

Centuries of Body Decoration

Body art has always been an important part of people's lives. Humans have painted, **tattooed**, and **pierced** their bodies throughout recorded history—and even before!

Ancient body painting and tattoos

Body paint and tattoos go back to the earliest recorded **cultures**. For example, scientists studying ancient humans in Africa found body paint they think is 400,000 years old. A 2,500-year-old mummy (preserved body) found in China has animal tattoos on his arm, shoulder, and back. In 54 BCE, Roman emperor Julius Caesar wrote about painted and tattooed **tribes** he saw living in northern Europe.

The Picts lived in Scotland during the time of the Roman Empire. Their name means "painted people."

Egypt, Greece, and Rome

About 4,000 years ago, Egyptian men and women shaved unwanted hair. Body oils were part of the wages paid to workers. Egyptian women wore eye makeup and colored their lips.

The ancient Greeks and Romans also experimented with body decoration. Around 500 BCE, Greek women used white lead (a kind of metal) to make their skin appear lighter. (Since then we have learned that lead can be poisonous.) Eye shadow and **rouge** were also popular. Greek and Roman women dyed their hair and wore wigs. About 2,000 years ago, Roman women used products to make their skin soft, including one made from crocodile **dung** (solid waste).

Nefertiti was the queen of Egypt around 1350 BCE. Notice the use of eye makeup in this statue of her.

Iranian beauty queen

In 2006 scientists working in Iran discovered women's items that were 5,000 years old. Among these items were a box for makeup, a comb, and a bowl and marble tool used for applying eyeliner.

A rebirth of body art

During the 1400s and 1500s, European explorers traveled to many distant places. Italian explorer Christopher Columbus sailed to the Americas in 1492, and English explorer Sir Francis Drake circled the globe from 1577 to 1580. Everywhere these explorers went, they discovered painted, tattooed, and pierced people. They brought new ideas about body art home with them.

Pale faces

Makeup became popular in Europe in the 1500s. Farmers and laborers had dark and rough skin from working in the sun. As a result queens—and kings—lightened their faces with pale paint and powder. This showed they were rich enough that they did not have to work outdoors. It also made them seem young and healthy.

In the 1500s, Queen Elizabeth I of England painted her skin white to create an image of purity. Her makeup became known as the "Mask of Youth."

Soon the upper classes started following this example. But the lower classes did not have time or money to spend on makeup.

Inked men

In the late 1700s, British explorer Captain James Cook made three voyages to the islands of the South Pacific. He described the tattooed people he saw and even brought one man back to England. Many of Cook's men, including his science officer, got tattooed. Over the next 100 years, tattooing spread throughout Europe.

This **Maori** chief lived around 1900. The tattoo on his face is called a **moko**.

Glamour shots

The growth of photography in the late 1800s helped popularize makeup. Women who refused to wear makeup in public would still lighten their skin and color their eyes, lips, and cheeks for photographs.

The Magic of Makeup and Hair

Makeup has come a long way since the lead paint and crocodile **dung** of the past. Today companies make billions of dollars from selling makeup. Makeup is worn by everyone from movie stars to people in your own family.

Makeup can be used both to hide flaws and to highlight facial features. Women, and sometimes men, use makeup to smooth out their skin, call attention to their lips and eyes, and color their fingernails and toenails.

Makeup products

Common makeup products include foundation, **rouge**, lipstick, and eye makeup such as eyeliner, eye shadow, and mascara. Foundation is used to smooth out the skin. Rouge, or blush, is used to color and highlight the cheeks, while lipstick colors the lips. Lipstick in a tube, which is most common today, first appeared in 1915.

FOR THAT S·M·O·O·T·H *Young* LOOK!

★ Add new, thrilling glamour to your looks right now . . . in just a few seconds . . . with "Pan-Cake" make-up, the famous glamorizing make-up originated by *Max Factor Hollywood*. You'll love the smooth, flawless, beautiful new complexion it creates for you . . . and you'll be delighted with the way it helps hide tiny skin faults. Try "Pan-Cake" make-up just once and you'll immediately discover why screen stars say that it is the greatest glamour make-up in the history of cosmetics.

ELLEN DREW Starring in COLUMBIA'S "THE SWORDSMAN"

PAN-CAKE BRAND MAKE-UP

MAX FACTOR 'Cosmetics of the Stars' are obtainable from your local Chemist, Hair-dresser & Store

Complete Your Make-up in Colour Harmony with *Max Factor Hollywood* Face Powder, Rouge and Lipstick.

Max Factor HOLLYWOOD

Polish-American makeup artist Max Factor designed makeup for many Hollywood stars. They then appeared in ads selling his products.

Versions of foundation, rouge, lipstick, and eye makeup have been around since the time of ancient Egypt, but mascara is the first modern makeup. Mascara is a kind of makeup used to color and thicken eyelashes. Its name came from the Italian word *maschera*, which means "mask." It was first sold in 1913.

Birth of fake lashes

U.S. film director D.W. Griffith invented false eyelashes in 1916. He was directing a movie and wanted his actress to have longer lashes. He had a wig maker attach human hair to pieces of thin fabric and then glue them to the actress's eyelids.

Fashion and makeup go together. This model's makeup highlights her clothing.

Hair-raising hair

Hair and makeup have always gone hand-in-hand. People dye their hair both natural and unusual colors. They may add length or body by adding hairpieces called weaves or extensions. Sometimes an entire head is covered with a wig.

Complex hairstyles reached their peak in France in the late 1700s. Hairdressers wove women's hair into wire frames that were sometimes 0.5 to 1 meter (2 to 3 feet) tall. Then they added fake hair, which they held in place with perfumed animal fat. Once the fat dried, the hair was cut into shapes and decorated with beads, fruit, and even live birds.

Since these styles were so expensive to have done, women kept them in place for weeks. By the end of that time, they smelled terrible and sometimes hid spiders— or worse. This might be why we say messy hair is like a rat's nest.

The French Queen Marie Antoinette (1755–1793) was known for her creative hairstyles.

Sing its praises

Advertising is an important part of selling beauty products. An important part of advertising is a catchy jingle, or song. Now it is your turn to write a jingle.

Steps to follow:

1. Come up with a product you want to sell. It could be something you have read about in this book, or something you make up, such as Marie Antoinette's Hair Bug Spray. Choose a product you find interesting or gross!

2. Come up with a tune. The easiest way is to use a popular tune or a children's song. For example, "Twinkle, Twinkle, Little Star" is simple and easy to remember.

3. Now decide on the words. What do you want to say about the product? Write down words that rhyme. For "hair" you might write, "air, fair, lair," and so on. Write down words that describe the product. For "bug spray" you might write, "spider, kill, bomb, dead."

4. Put it all together. If you wrote a jingle for hair bug spray using "Twinkle, Twinkle," you might write this:
   Marie's Bug Spray for your hair
   Kills the spiders if you dare.

Share your jingles. See who has the catchiest tune—or the funniest!

Have fun sharing your jingles. Use your face and body to help sell your product.

Kathakali is a kind of dance-drama from India. The colors of the makeup have meaning. Green is used for noble characters, while evil characters have red faces and a red beard.

Stage makeup

Stage makeup is much darker than regular makeup, to help performers' faces stand out under the bright stage lights. Actors use makeup to shape their face. They highlight areas they want to stand out and shadow areas they want to make appear deeper. They can create wrinkles and jowls (loose skin), making a young actor appear much older.

In Asian countries such as China, India, and Japan, performers paint themselves in bright colors that are not realistic. In **Kabuki**, a Japanese form of musical drama, human characters have pure-white faces. Other colors show the characters' age, gender, and mood. Characters with pink lines on their face are young and happy, while characters painted deep blue are gloomy.

Am I blue?

The Blue Man Group is a stage show that combines music, comedy, and media such as video. The three performers wear black costumes and blue makeup that covers their entire faces and heads. In this show, makeup is used to make the actors all look alike, rather than different.

From stage to home

Stage makeup helped spark an interest in makeup among the public. In 1911 the Ballet Russes, a famous Russian ballet company, performed in London, England. The dancers wore striking makeup, especially makeup that highlighted their eyes. Sales of eyeliner and colored eye shadow then exploded, as women tried to copy the dancers' makeup.

The individual performers of the Blue Man Group disappear beneath their makeup.

Body Painting

Body painting is different from makeup. While people wear makeup to appear more beautiful or to play a part, body paint has deeper meanings.

Transformation

Tribal people often paint their bodies as part of a **ceremony**, such as initiations (ceremonies where people join a group), weddings, and funerals. The paint transforms, or changes, the person from an individual to something more, such as a member of a group or a married woman. Body paint is also seen as a kind of protection, which is why some warriors wear it going into battle.

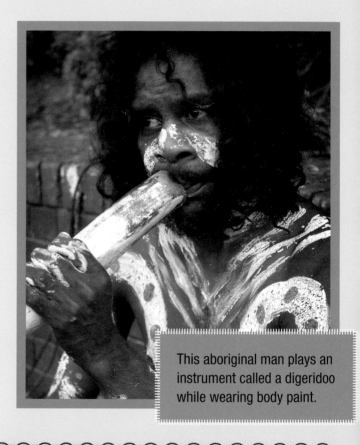

This aboriginal man plays an instrument called a digeridoo while wearing body paint.

Scientists have found red and black body paints made from minerals, such as iron, that are 75,000 years old. Tribal people today make their paint from seeds, fruits, or colored clay. The pigment, or color, is then mixed with oil or animal fat.

Team spirit

Some fans at sporting events paint their faces and bodies in the colors of their favorite team. They feel like tribal warriors!

Temporary tattoos

Body paint is used to create temporary (not lasting) tattoos, which are a safe alternative to real tattoos. **Mehndi** is a popular form of temporary tattooing from India. In mehndi, a reddish-brown dye called henna is applied to the skin using a paintbrush or a tool called a stylus. Mehndi tattoos are usually very complex.

Mehndi tattoos are traditionally used as part of wedding ceremonies in India. The dye can last from a week to several months.

Face painting

Like body painting, face painting often has meaning beyond decoration. Native Americans painted their faces to give them more power in battle or hunting. They believed the paint would help them draw power from the world around them. Different colors had special meanings. For example, they wore green paint under their eyes to give them better vision at night.

Ancient and modern soldiers paint their face for **camouflage**. They use colors of the surrounding environment, such as green and brown, to make themselves difficult to see. Hunters sometimes use camouflage, too.

Today, face painting is popular with children and adults at fairs and festivals. Artists use special paints to draw pictures directly onto people's faces. This face painting is just for fun.

Paint your face!

Face painting can be a fun activity. Be sure that you only use face paints provided by an adult.

Steps to follow:

1. First, choose a design. You can find ideas in books and comics, or search for ideas online. Animals, clowns, and superheroes are popular. Keep your first design simple.

2. Use a computer printout or a photocopy of a face to plan your ideas. Try designs that follow the shape of the face. Repeating patterns, like tiger stripes or leopard spots, can be fun. Keep drawing until you get a design you like.

3. Assemble your supplies. Sponges are used to apply paint to a large area. Brushes are used for detailed work.

4. It is time to paint! Painting someone else's face is easier than painting your own, so you might want to do this with a friend or in a group.

You and your friends can paint your faces as part of a group project. For example, you might all be different animals in a zoo.

Don't worry if your painting isn't perfect. As long as it's colorful, no one will know.

Body painting as fine art

Some artists have turned body painting into a fine art, meaning they explore it simply for the sake of beauty. Instead of painting on a canvas, they paint their work directly onto a human model.

The painting may cover one part of a model's body, or it may cover the entire body. Some artists paint the model's body so that he or she disappears into the background. This is an extreme kind of camouflage!

Living statues

In big cities, performers work as "living statues." They paint their bodies to look like stone or metal and wear a costume that is the same color. Part of the fun is surprising passersby, who do not know they are actually people. Living statues are also popular at parties.

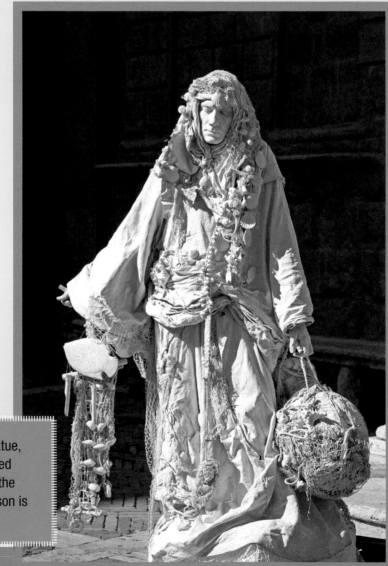

Though this looks like a statue, it is actually a person painted to look like one. People on the street do not know the person is alive until he moves!

Make a human artwork

Living statues turn their bodies into a piece of art. You and your friends can use your bodies and voices to create a living artwork called a "human machine." When you build your machine, think about the moving parts in factory machines and amusement park rides.

Steps to follow:

1. One person repeats a motion and a sound that goes with it. For example, you might thrust your arms forward and back, making a different sound for each movement. Don't think too much about it—just have fun!

2. Now another person joins in with a different movement and sound. This person should build on the movement of the first person. For example, the second person might put his or her hands in the air when the first person pushes his or her arms forward.

3. One by one, have other friends join in. Each new person should try to connect with one or more part of the "machine."

4. What is your machine's name? Be creative! What you can make is only limited by your imagination.

Have other people watch your machine. Ask them what they think it does!

As more people become part of the machine, it becomes more fun. Try to all move together, just like a real machine.

Tattooing

Tattoos are designs or pictures that are **permanently** inked into the skin. People around the world wear tattoos. The various **tribes** Captain Cook met (see page 9) wore tattoos on their faces. Today it is more common for people to get tattoos on their arms, legs, and other parts of their bodies.

Tattoos have many meanings

In some **cultures**, a tattoo was a sign of an important life experience. People got tattoos when they became an adult, as a reward for bravery, or as part of a religious **ceremony**.

Many modern tattoos are based on designs worn by **tribal** people in the Pacific Islands and Asia. People who wear these tattoos often simply like the design, rather than feeling connected to the original meaning.

Today most people get tattoos to express some part of their personality. They may also get a tattoo to show that they are a member of a group, or to show their connection to a culture.

How tattoos work

Tattoos are made by using needles to **inject** dyes under the skin, into the layer of flesh called the dermis. Because the dyes are injected beneath the skin, the pattern does not fade as the top layer of skin wears away. A modern tattoo machine can drive needles into the skin up to 3,000 times a minute!

Tattoo artists

Skilled tattoo artists may train with a teacher for five years or more before they are ready to tattoo on their own. Tattoo designs can take hours to complete. Tattoo artists protect their customers by working in **sanitary** (clean) conditions.

Not only do tattoo artists create art—they do it on living skin!

Piercing

During **piercing** a hole is made in the body with a needle. Then a piece of jewelry is put through the hole. After the hole heals, it is easy to take the jewelry out and put it back in. Rings and rods are the most common jewelry used.

Many piercings, many reasons

Many **cultures** practice body piercing. Ears and noses are pierced most often. In some cultures, piercings have special meaning. For example, in India infants have their ears pierced as part of a religious **ceremony**.

In Europe during the 1500s, both men and women wore earrings. By the 1900s, earrings were mostly worn by women. In Western countries, men mostly wore earrings to be rebellious. Today, it is fairly common among both women and men.

English playwright William Shakespeare (1564–1616) had his ears pierced, as did many other men of his day.

Piercings everywhere

The most common body part to get pierced is the ear. Instead of just piercing earlobes, people now put piercings through many different parts of their ears.

Pierced noses, lips, and even tongues have followed as areas to be pierced. "Surface piercings" go through any loose piece of skin, such as the eyebrow.

"Stretching" has also become popular in recent years. People place wide rods, called plugs, through their piercings. Over time, they stretch the holes with larger and larger plugs. Once stretched, these holes will never close up.

Too many?

Elaine Davidson of Scotland holds the title of the Most Pierced Woman in the World. She has more than 6,000 piercings.

Some people stretch their piercings using large plugs.

The Other Side of Body Art

Many people do not like body art. They may think someone who has many **tattoos** and **piercings** is immature and cannot be trusted. Some people link piercings and tattoos with criminal activity.

Workplace problems

Many companies will not hire people who have piercings and tattoos. They may allow women to wear earrings, but only in their earlobes. Men may not be allowed to wear any piercings. Both men and women may need to cover their tattoos. Some jobs require men and women to remove jewelry worn in piercings because of safety concerns.

Many schools also have rules about the kinds of piercing and tattoos students may wear. These attitudes are changing, but not quickly.

Some people may find this man's tattoos and piercings threatening.

Dangers of piercing

Body piercing can create some health risks. Some people have **allergic** reactions to products used to clean the piercing, or even to the metal in the jewelry. **Infections** can occur during the piercing or healing process, especially if the conditions are not **sanitary**. Lip piercings can injure the gums underneath. Because of these risks, people should only get piercings from qualified professionals.

A pierced ear can take weeks to heal. During this time, it is important to keep the piercing clean.

Removing tattoos

Almost 20 percent of people who get tattoos change their mind later in life. Tattoos can be removed using lasers. It usually takes many sessions and can be very painful. Even then, complete removal is not guaranteed.

Looking to the Future

Science and design are working together to create new kinds of body art. Some of these methods are **temporary**, while others involve surgery.

Body implants

An extreme form of body art places **implants** under the skin. In some cases, the skin heals over the implants, leaving raised patterns in the skin. Other times, spikes, horns, or other ornaments are attached to the implants.

Permanent makeup

Today, some women wear **permanent** makeup. They have eyeliner **tattooed** onto their eyelids and have color **injected** into their lips.

What next?

The future of body art is impossible to predict. Plastic surgery, in which people alter their physical appearance, is common. In 2010 a team of surgeons in Spain successfully performed the first full face transplant. This surgery was done to repair damage from an accident, but it opens the door to new possibilities. Scientists are also currently experimenting with ways to tint eyes and skin.

Since the beginning of time, human beings have decorated their bodies. This is not likely to change. Only time will tell what kinds of body decoration will come with new technologies.

The future

In the future, people may reshape their bodies in many ways. This woman had her ears reshaped by a doctor. Implants under her skin created a new ridge above her eyes. Fat injected into her lips made them larger and fuller. Her skin and eyes have been tinted new colors. She also has tattoos that make her look like she has scales.

Glossary

allergic becoming sick or getting a rash from something

camouflage coloring that allows something to blend in with the background. A tiger's stripes are a natural form of camouflage.

ceremony formal event that has meaning for people. A graduation is a ceremony students are happy to go through.

culture group of people who share a common background, traditions, and way of life. Every country has its own culture.

dung solid waste created by an animal. An elephant produces a lot of dung.

implant object that is placed under the skin. Some people have implants added to their bodies as a form of body art.

infection a disease caused by germs

inject to put something under the skin

Kabuki classical Japanese musical drama. Kabuki plays are not realistic and sometimes last for several hours.

Kathakali a traditional play with music and dance performed in India

Maori native people of New Zealand

mehndi method of painting designs on hands and feet. Mehndi was originally used to paint a bride before her wedding.

moko permanent face and body marks worn by Maori people

permanent lasting forever. Tattoos are made with permanent ink.

pierce make a hole in something. When you get your ear pierced, a needle is pushed though your earlobe.

rouge red makeup used on the cheeks. Women with rosy cheeks sometimes are wearing rouge.

sanitary clean and free from germs

soot ash that's left after a fire

tattoo design that is inked into the skin. The word is also used to describe the act of creating this design in the skin.

temporary lasting for a short time. Temporary tattoos wash off after a short time.

tribal people, art, or activities belonging to a tribe

tribe an organized group of people who live together and share beliefs and activities

Find Out More

Books

Gottesman, Eric. *Classic Tattoo Designs Coloring Book*. Mineola, N.Y.: Dover, 2006.

Henry de Tessan, Christina. *Makeup Artist Studio*. Bellevue, Wash.: SmartLab, 2009.

Levin, Judith. *Tattoos and Indigenous Peoples*. New York: Rosen, 2009.

Websites

Teens Health
http://kidshealth.org/teen/your_body/
This website provides lots of good health information for kids and teens. Tattoos and body piercing are covered in the "Body Art" section of the site.

American Museum of Natural History Body Art Exhibit
http://www.amnh.org/exhibitions/bodyart/
Learn about body art and its history from this website.

Place to see body art

Face and Body Art International Convention
Orlando, Florida
www.fabaic.com
This event takes place every May. Visit the website to find out more details and see photos.

Index

activities 13, 19, 21
advertising 13
Africa 6
arthritis 5

Ballet Russes 15
Blue Man Group 15
body painting 4, 6, 8, 16, 17, 20

Caesar, Julius 6
camouflage 18, 20
ceremonies 4, 16, 22, 24
China 6, 14
Columbus, Christopher 8
Cook, James 9, 22

Davidson, Elaine 25
dermis 23
Drake, Sir Francis 8

England 15
Europe 6, 8, 12, 24
extensions 12
eye makeup 7, 9, 10, 11, 15, 28

face painting 8, 14, 15, 16, 18, 19
face transplants 29
false eyelashes 11
foundation 10, 11
France 12
future 29

Greece 7
Griffith, D.W. 11

hair 4, 7, 12
health risks 27
henna 17
history 6, 7, 8, 9, 10, 11, 12, 15, 16, 18, 22, 24

implants 28
India 14, 17
Iran 7

Japan 14

Kabuki performers 14

lipstick 10, 11
living statues 20, 21

makeup 4, 7, 8, 9, 10–11, 12, 14, 15, 28
mascara 10, 11
mehndi tattoos 17
mummies 5, 6

Native Americans 18

photography 9
piercings 4, 8, 24, 25, 26, 27
plugs 25
public opinion 26

Rome 6, 7
Russia 15

safety 17, 23, 26, 27
sporting events 16
stage makeup 14, 15
"stretching" 25
South Pacific Islands 9
surface piercings 25

tattoos 4, 5, 6, 8, 9, 17, 22–23, 26, 27
temporary tattoos 17
tribal people 6, 9, 16, 18, 22

weaves 12
wigs 7, 12